# LOVE FOR A LIFETIME
## BIBLE STUDY
### BUILDING A MARRIAGE THAT WILL GO THE DISTANCE

# DR. JAMES DOBSON

developed with Michael O'Neal

LifeWay Press®
Nashville, Tennessee

Published by LifeWay Press®
© 2014 Siggie, LLC

*Love for a Lifetime* © 2015 by Dr. James Dobson. Published by Tyndale House Publishers;
Carol Stream, IL. Used by Permission.

ISBN: 978-1-4300-3301-1
Item: 005650402

Dewey decimal classification: 306.81
Subject headings: MARRIAGE \ HUSBANDS \ WIVES

Unless indicated otherwise, all Scripture quotations are taken from the Holman Christian Standard Bible.
Copyright © 1999, 2000, 2002, 2003, 2009 by Holman Bible Publishers. Used by permission. Holman
Christian Standard Bible® and HCSB® are federally registered trademarks of Holman Bible Publishers.

Cover photo: Randy Hughes/LifeWay Photo.

To order additional copies of this resource, write to LifeWay Church Resources, Customer Service,
One LifeWay Plaza, Nashville, TN 37234-0113; fax 615.251.5933; phone 800.458.2772; order online
at *www.lifeway.com* or email *orderentry@lifeway.com;* or visit the LifeWay Christian Store serving you.

Printed in the United States of America

Adult Ministry Publishing, LifeWay Church Resources, One LifeWay Plaza, Nashville, TN 37234-0152

# Contents

## WEEK 1

## WEEK 2

## WEEK 3

## WEEK 4

# About the Author

**DR. JAMES DOBSON** is the founder and president of Family Talk, a nonprofit organization that produces his radio program, "Dr. James Dobson's Family Talk." He is the author of more than 50 books dedicated to the preservation of the family, including *The New Dare to Discipline; Love for a Lifetime: Building a Marriage That Will Go the Distance; Life on the Edge; Love Must Be Tough; The New Strong-Willed Child; When God Doesn't Make Sense; Bringing Up Boys; Bringing Up Girls; Head Over Heels;* and, most recently, *Dr. Dobson's Handbook of Family Advice.*

Dr. Dobson served as an associate clinical professor of pediatrics at the University of Southern California School of Medicine for fourteen years and on the attending staff of Children's Hospital of Los Angeles for seventeen years in the divisions of Child Development and Medical Genetics. He has been active in governmental affairs and has advised three United States presidents on family matters.

In 1967 he earned his PhD in child development from the University of Southern California and holds eighteen honorary doctoral degrees. In 2009 he was inducted into the National Radio Hall of Fame.

Dr. Dobson and his wife, Shirley, reside in Colorado Springs, Colorado. They have two grown children, Danae and Ryan, and two grandchildren.

**MICHAEL O'NEAL** is minister of education and missions at First Baptist Church, Cumming, Georgia. He has also served as youth minister, worship leader, associate pastor, church planter, and college/seminary professor. He and his wife, Carrie, are parents to two boys.

# How to Use This Study

The four sessions of this study may be used weekly or during a weekend retreat. But we recommend that before you dig into this material, you watch the film *Love for a Lifetime* from the *Dr. James Dobson Presents: Building a Family Legacy* film series. This will lay the groundwork for your study.

This material has been written for a small-group experience, for you and your spouse to do together, or for personal study.

An option to extend or conclude this study is for your group to view the film *Your Legacy* from the *Dr. James Dobson Presents: Building a Family Legacy* film series.

**CONNECT:** The purpose of the introductory section of each session invites and motivates you to connect with the topic of the session and others in your group.

**WATCH:** The study DVD contains four DVD clips which include introductions from Ryan Dobson and clips from a talk by Dr. James Dobson, based on the film and the accompanying book *Love for a Lifetime* (Tyndale Momentum; ISBN 978-1-4964-0328-5) by Dr. Dobson.

**ENGAGE:** This section is the primary focus of each week's group time. You and other participants will further engage the truths of Scripture and discuss accompanying questions. This section will also include a Wrap-Up portion, which concludes the group session and leads to the Reflect section.

**REFLECT:** This at-home study section helps you dig deeper into Scripture and apply the truths you're learning. Go deeper each week by reading the suggested chapters in the book *Love for a Lifetime* and completing the activities at the end of each session in this study.

# Guidelines for Groups

While you can complete this study alone, you will benefit greatly from covering the material with your spouse or with the interaction of a Sunday School class or small group. Here are a few ways to cultivate a valuable experience as you engage in this study.

**PREPARATION:** To get the most out of each group time, read through the study each week and answer the questions so you're ready to discuss the material. It will also be helpful for you and your group members to have copies of the book *Love for a Lifetime* (ISBN 978-1-4964-0328-5). Read it in advance of the study to prepare, and encourage your members to read the corresponding chapters each week. In your group, don't let one or two people shoulder the entire responsibility for conversation and participation. Everyone can pitch in and contribute.

**CONFIDENTIALITY:** In the study, you will be prompted to share thoughts, feelings, and personal experiences. Accept others where they are without judgment. Many of the challenges discussed will be private. These should be kept in strict confidence by the group.

**RESPECT:** Participants must respect each other's thoughts and opinions, providing a safe place for those insights to be shared without fear of judgment or unsolicited advice (including hints, sermons, instructions, and scriptural Band-Aids®). Take off your fix-it hat and leave it at the door, so you can just listen. If advice is requested, then it's okay to lend your opinion, seasoned with grace and offered with love.

**ACCOUNTABILITY:** Each week, participants will be challenged to make their love for the Lord and their love for their spouse their highest priorities. Commit to supporting and encouraging each other during the sessions and praying for each other between meetings.

# Introduction

The statistics are disheartening. When I wrote *Love for a Lifetime* in 1987 just over one million couples divorced that year in the United States.[1] The average duration of first marriages was only eight years.[2] A study in 2012 indicated that only half of married couples will celebrate their 20th anniversary.[3]

Is there hope? Yes ... a resounding yes.

My parents and grandparents modeled a love that lasted a lifetime. After more than 50 years of marriage to Shirley, I believe that a fulfilling, enduring marriage is possible. Not only for us, but for you, too.

So what can we learn from couples whose marriages are healthy and long lasting?

I asked husbands and wives who have been married at least 10 years, "What do you think are key ingredients to a healthy, long-lasting marriage?" Here are a few of their responses:

- "After 15 years, my wife and I enjoy spending time together. We are still best friends."
- "I believe the proposition that marriage is 50/50 is incorrect. It is 100/100. Both husband and wife must choose to love and to give all they have to one another."
- "The key ingredients are putting her thoughts, feelings, and interests ahead of my own."
- "We know that God makes us one but we are still individuals created with different personalities."
- "Love God. He will give me a love for my spouse that will keep our marriage healthy and lasting a lifetime."

All of these couples undoubtedly have experienced tough times together, but they continue to love each other in and through life's circumstances and challenges. The purpose of this study is to equip and encourage you as you seek to have a God-honoring marriage. In our time together, we will address such questions as:

- What are God-given responsibilities of husbands and wives?
- With life's demands and busy schedules, how is it possible to make time for your spouse?
- What does it look like for couples to both love God and love each other?
- What is a biblical view of money, and how can couples use their money wisely and generously?

Next to your relationship with God, your relationship with your spouse must take the highest priority. It is more important than your relationship with your kids, your parents, or any other person in your life.

During this four-week journey, I pray that God will strengthen and cultivate your relationship with Him and with your spouse.

1. Divorce, Provisional 1998 data. National Center for Health Statistics [online]. Available from the Internet: http//www.cdc.gov/nchs/fastats/divorce.html. Cited 13 January 2003 in *Love for a Lifetime: Building a Marriage That Will Go the Distance* (Multnomah Gifts, a division of Random House: 2003), 17.
2. "Number, Timing, and Duration of Marriages and Divorces: 2001," *U.S. Census* [online], February 2005 [cited 9 June 2014]. Available from the Internet: *www.census.gov*.
3. "Why your first marriage has a 50 percent chance of lasting," *Fox News* [online], 23 March 2012 (cited 16 May 2014). Available from the Internet: *http://www.foxnews.com/health/2012/03/23/why-your-1st-marriage-has-a-50-percent-chance-lasting/*.

WEEK 1

# OPPOSITES
# ATTRACT

● **BEFORE YOU BEGIN,** take time to pray with your group. Ask God to strengthen your own marriage and the marriages of each member of your group.

As you begin this four-week journey together, take a few minutes to get acquainted.

Tell the group a little about yourself (name, family, where you grew up, how you met (please be brief!), and how long you have been married).

Share what you hope to learn from this study.

Newlyweds have lots to learn about how to live together as husband and wife. Newly married couples quickly discover: How are we going to balance work and together time? Where will we attend church together? Who will manage the money? Who will buy the groceries, who will do the dishes, and who will replace the toilet paper roll?

What were some of the funny things you discovered about your spouse when you were first married?

How are you and your spouse different? What do you appreciate about those differences?

**WATCH CLIP 1** from the study DVD and answer the following questions:

From my extensive marital and psychological counseling, I became aware that depression plagued more women than men. Discovering emerging patterns, I developed a *Sources of Depression in Women* survey.

I asked seventy-five women to rank certain variables from the most to the least troublesome to them. This list reflects their ratings.

1. Low self-esteem
2. Fatigue and time pressure
3. Loneliness, isolation, and boredom (as one item) and Absence of romantic love in marriage
4. Financial difficulties
5. Sexual problems in marriage
6. Menstrual and physiological problems
7. Problems with the children
8. Aging

Does it surprise you that low self-esteem was the number-one factor in depression? Why or why not?

Highlight two or three factors that you think might be sources of depression among married women today. Add these to the list above.

Men primarily develop their self-esteem from their work. Women, however, whether staying at home or working outside the home, tend to develop their self-esteem based on their relationships, especially with their husbands. To know your spouse's needs is essential to a healthy marriage.

What will it take for you to help your spouse identify those needs? What can you do to assure your spouse that you care?

● **CONTINUE YOUR GROUP TIME** with this discussion guide.

Imagine it's halftime at the Super Bowl. One team's coach makes a game-changing decision. The middle linebacker is going to play quarterback in the second half. What do you think will happen?

At the very least, the change will distract the team and hurt their chance of winning. After all, the linebacker is responsible for tackling opposing ball carriers and the quarterback's job is to call plays and distribute the ball. It's "game over" as soon as the linebacker forsakes his responsibility and takes on a role he is not meant to play.

Many couples experience "game over" by failing to recognize and accept their God-given roles and responsibilities. Scripture gives husbands and wives God's perfect game plan.

● **READ** Ephesians 5:22-33.

After reading these words from the apostle Paul, move into separate husband-wife discussion groups.

> **WIVES:** When women read or hear the word *submit*, what might they think it means? What might some men think it means?

The Holman Christian Standard Study Bible provides this excellent commentary on Paul's exhortation for wives to voluntarily submit to their husbands: "No external coercion should be involved, nor should submission imply that the wife is a lesser partner in the marital union. The submission is governed by the phrase *as to the Lord*. Christian wives' submission to their husbands is one dimension of their obedience to Christ. Submission is a person's yielding his or her own rights and losing self for another. Submission is patterned after Christ's example and reflects the essence of the gospel. (See Phil. 2:5-8.) Submission distinguishes the lifestyle of all Christians."[1]

Based on these ideas, talk about what a wife's submission should look like. Why is this type of submission necessary for a healthy marriage?

Consider some practical day-to-day ways submission expresses itself: "Submission is the divine calling of a wife to honor and affirm her husband's leadership and help carry it through according to her gifts. It's the disposition to follow a husband's authority and an inclination to yield to his leadership. It is an attitude that says, 'I delight for you to take the initiative in our family. I am glad when you take responsibility for things and lead with love. I don't flourish in the relationship when you are passive and I have to make sure the family works.' "[2]

How does Ephesians 5:25 put submission into its proper context?

● **READ** 1 Peter 3:1-2 for one outcome of godly submission.

Wives, submit yourselves to your own husbands so that, even if some disobey the Christian message, they may be won over without a message by the way their wives live when they observe your pure, reverent lives.

**WIVES:** What can you do to make sure your husband sees Christ revealed in the way you live?

What can you do to support and inspire your husband to be the spiritual leader of your family?

Men have the God-given responsibility to love their wives sacrificially.

**HUSBANDS**: What does it look like for a husband to love his wife with Christ-like, sacrificial love? How does having your wife's respect encourage you as spiritual leader of your home?

The God-given responsibility to lead spiritually includes encouraging your wife to grow in her faith and a commitment to meet her needs.

In what ways can you encourage your wife to grow in her personal faith?

Low self-esteem is still a struggle among many women. Wives need affirmation, to be appreciated and valued by their husbands. They also want their husbands to spend quality time with the family.

What can you say and do to affirm and appreciate your wife?

How can you be more intentional about putting your family before work and other activities? Be specific.

# THIS WEEK'S INSIGHTS

• • •

- Husbands and wives have distinctive God-ordained roles and responsibilities in marriage.
- Submission means yielding one's rights for another person.
- Husbands are to love sacrificially and lead spiritually, following Christ's example as head of the church.
- Wives are to give themselves to their husbands, respecting and meeting their needs, just as the church submits to Christ. They find encouragement in their husband's affirmation and support.

This week what are ways you can apply Ephesians 5:33 and so reflect love and respect for your spouse?

# WRAP UP

• • •

**PRAY TOGETHER** as a group, that each participant would stay connected to God and each other. Read Romans 5:8: "But God proves His own love for us in that while we were still sinners, Christ died for us!" Spend a few moments thanking God for His Son.

Holy, loving Father, In Your providence, You have brought us together. Thank You for my spouse and family and for how You want to use us in Your Kingdom.

Lead us during the normal days and the challenging ones. Help us to fulfill our God-given responsibilities to each other. Thank You that Your Son has met our greatest need—for forgiveness and reconciliation.

● **READ AND COMPLETE** the activities for this section before your next group time. For details on the Sources of Depression in Women survey, see *What Wives Wish Their Husbands Knew About Women.*

## A WIFE'S GREATEST NEED

Husbands, how can we help our wives see themselves as God sees them and base their self esteem in Him?

Joyce Landorf Heatherly, the author of *His Stubborn Love*, once asked me: What would you change about women in general if you could wave some sort of magic wand? I answered,

> If I could write a prescription for the women of the world, I would provide each one of them with a healthy dose of self-esteem and personal worth (taken three times a day until the symptoms disappear). ... If women felt genuinely respected in their role as wives and mothers, they would not need to abandon it for something better. If they felt equal with men in personal worth, they would not need to be equivalent to men in responsibility. If they could only bask in the dignity and status granted them by the Creator, then their femininity would be valued as their greatest asset rather than scorned as an old garment to be discarded.[3]

We saw in the *Sources of Depression in Women*, many wives and mothers , when given the opportunity to privately reflect their true feelings, experience self-doubt and insecurity. These women may be outwardly social and pleasant, even laughing and interacting, yet they experience a sense of inferiority they wish their husbands understood about them.

# FUNDAMENTALS OF
# CHRISTIAN MARRIAGE

In another study, approximately 600 married couples were asked to share key marriage principles that had worked for them. Three overarching principles emerged.

**1. A CHRIST-CENTERED HOME.** Everything rests on the foundation of a personal relationship with Jesus and a meaningful prayer life. For Shirley and me, this communication between man, woman, and God has been *the* stabilizing factor in our 50-plus years of married life.

The couple that depends on Scripture for solutions to the questions and stresses of living has a distinct advantage over the family with no faith. The Bible we love is the world's most incredible text. By reading these Holy Scriptures we are given a window into the mind of the Father.

**2. COMMITTED LOVE.** A marriage built on committed love is secure to defend against the inevitable storms of life. What will you do when unexpected tempests blow through your home or when the doldrums leave your sails sagging and silent? Will you quit? Will you retreat or seek ways to strike back? Or will your commitment hold steady? You must answer these questions before Satan has an opportunity to discourage you. Set your resolve now. Nothing short of death must ever be permitted to come between the two of you.

**3. COMMUNICATION.** Most little girls are blessed with greater linguistic ability than most little boys, and communication and expression remains a lifelong talent for them. As an adult, a woman typically expresses her feeling and thoughts far better than her husband and is often irritated by his reticence to openly talk.

The inability or unwillingness of husbands to reveal their feelings to their wives is one of the most common complaints wives have. Men tend to only engage in conversations that have a destination. "What time should I be there?" "When is Johnny's dentist appointment?"

Women often engage in talk that has no specific goal ... other than relationship building.

Compromise, as always, is needed. As a gesture of love and out of obedience to Christ, a man may need to press himself to open his heart and share his feelings with his wife. Time must be reserved for meaningful conversations. In time, most men will find that this special time is well worth it. For women, especially full-time homemakers with small children, having girlfriends with whom they can talk heart to heart, study the Scriptures, and share childcare techniques can be vital to her mental health and marriage.

# HUSBANDS: LAYING DOWN YOUR LIFE

To be the spiritual leader of your home means taking the initiative. Laying down your life for your wife. Sacrificing yourself by putting her needs before your own. Showing her what it means to live a holy, godly life, not just talking about it. Leading out spiritually.

R. Kent Hughes, author of *Disciplines of a Godly Man*, challenges husbands to take spiritual leadership in these ways:

1. **PROMOTE HER HOLINESS.** While we cannot make our wives holy, we certainly can help them pursue holiness. Ask yourself: *Is my wife more or less like Christ because she is married to me?*[4]

2. **PURSUE HOLINESS IN YOUR OWN LIFE.** The way to earn your wife's trust and respect is to pursue holiness yourself. First Thessalonians 4:3-5 makes it clear that holiness (quickly confessing sin and living a life that is transparent) is what God demands from us.

3. **PROVIDE FOR HER NEEDS.** While your wife needs your appreciation and affirmation, she also needs your faithfulness. Set and keep clear personal boundaries in order to be faithful to her, no matter what situation you may encounter.

Husbands, this month, determine something you will do for each of the following:

- Encourage your wife's holiness.
- Pursue holiness in your own life.
- Seek to meet your wife's needs.

## WIVES: APPLYING 1 PETER 3:1-2

Wives, what do you do when your husband is not fulfilling his God-given responsibility at home? Believers in the early church were asking the same question.

● **READ** 1 Peter 3:1-2.

Accepting your husband's authority does not mean you are less valuable in the relationship. It does not mean you must do everything he says. It simply means that as you interact with him on a daily basis, you have a respectful, humble attitude regarding his leadership.

These words should be an encouragement. If you live a godly life, a life of devotion to God, a life of trust in God and respect for your husband, then God may use you to change your husband—to win him over from being self-centered to living a Christ-centered life.

**1. PURSUE HOLINESS IN EVERY AREA OF YOUR LIFE.** Certainly there should be a difference between the lifestyle of a Christian and that of a non-Christian. Peter challenged the early church with these words: "So you must live as God's obedient children. Don't slip back into your old ways of living to satisfy your own desires. You didn't know any better then. But now you must be holy in everything you do, just as God who chose you is holy. For the Scriptures say, 'You must be holy because I am holy' " (1 Pet. 1:14-16, NLT).

Wives, your husbands are watching. Husbands, your wives are watching. Parents, your children are watching. Your neighbors are also watching. When the world sees something in us that they don't have, when they see the difference Christ makes in our lives, then they will want what we have. Pursue holiness in every area of your life.

**2. SERVE THE NEEDS OF YOUR HUSBAND.** Ask God to help you serve your husband willingly and lovingly. If he is not yet a follower of Christ, don't judge him. A woman can be a blessing to her husband by honoring him in the same way as the church honors Christ. Evaluate the extent to which you are meeting your husband's need for:

- Your admiration and respect.
- Sexual fulfillment.
- Support at home.
- Taking care of your appearance.
- Being his best friend.[5]

## PERSONAL REFLECTION
• • •

Spend some time this week reflecting on this question:

### How do my spouse and I base our marriage on the fundamentals of Christian marriage?

1. Ephesians 5:22-33, *The Holman Christian Standard Study Bible* (online) [cited 16 May 2014]. Available from the Internet: *http://www.mystudybible.com/*.
2. John Piper, "The Beautiful Faith of Fearless Submission," *Desiring God* (online), 15 April 2007 [cited 16 May 2014]. Available from the Internet: *http://www.desiringgod.org/resource-library/ sermons/the-beautiful-faith-of-fearless-submission*.
3. James C. Dobson, *What Wives Wish Their Husbands Knew About Women* (Carol Stream, IL: Tyndale House Publishers, 2003), 35.
4. R. Kent Hughes, *Disciplines of a Godly Man*, rev. ed. (Wheaton, IL: Crossway Books, 2001), 38.
5. Daniel Akin, "God on Marriage" (online) [cited 26 May 2014]. Available from the Internet: *http:// www.danielakin.com/wp-content/uploads/2009/04/family-life-seminar-half-manual.pdf*.

WEEK 2

# RUNNING ON
# EMPTY

● **START YOUR GROUP TIME** by discussing what participants discovered in their Reflect homework.

The stress level of adults in North America continues to rise. According to one study, more than 40 percent of adults admit their stress has increased over the past five years.[1] This stress, of course, affects their marriages, often causing fatigue and conflict.

> Why do you think so many married couples battle stress? What are some ways they try to handle it?

Would you agree that our society encourages hectic schedules and hurried lives? We have an appointment downtown. A deadline to meet. We need to get the kids to ball games and birthday parties. We are serving at a church event. We have a family gathering we must attend.

If we are honest, we all struggle with how to balance work, family, and other aspects of life, and this struggle frequently leads to a stress-filled marriage and home.

So what are husbands and wives to do? What can we do to keep from being consumed with daily challenges? How can we keep our relationship with our spouse a priority? In this week's session, we will look at biblical and practical answers to these relevant questions.

> As you consider all that your spouse does for you and your family, how can you help your mate handle life's daily pressures?

**WATCH CLIP 2** from the study DVD. Answer the following questions in groups of men or women:

In my research, men seem to be able to tolerate overcommitted schedules better than many women do.

> **To what extent do you find this true in your own marriage?**

Especially when children are young, parents spend most of their time focused on their care: feeding them, playing with them, helping them with homework, and so forth. Yet your marriage still requires that you and your spouse spend quality—and quantity—time together.

A healthy sex life is essential to a strong marriage. Yet, as we discovered in the video, men and women approach sexuality differently.

> **HUSBANDS: Your wife desires your attention and conversation. How can you spend quality time with her in a way that she recognizes and needs?**

> **WIVES: Your husband is more visually-oriented than you are and responds to physical attractiveness. How do you need to make sex a priority in a way that he recognizes and needs?**

● **CONTINUE YOUR GROUP TIME** with this discussion guide.

Throughout every season of life, we have opportunities to do good things. We can get involved in community activities. Serve faithfully in the church. Work hard and put in extra hours at the office. We play sports, spend time with friends, travel.

There is nothing wrong with these things. But too often we are so busy doing good things that we miss out on doing the best thing. And if we fail to do the best thing, then we find ourselves worried, stressed, and tired. God doesn't want us to fill our lives with a "bunch of stuff" (even if it's good stuff), only to miss out on the best thing we can do.

So as a couple, what is the best thing you can do for your marriage? Let's look at a passage in Luke 10 for insights. While it is a story of two sisters, this story teaches a lesson that applies to our marriages.

● **READ** Luke 10:38-42.

> What does this story teach us about Martha? About Mary? About Jesus?

> In verse 42, what does Jesus mean when He tells Martha that one thing is necessary and that Mary has made the right choice? (See v. 39.) Men, how does this story bother you? Women, what do you like about this story? Why?

The "one thing necessary" was sitting at the feet of Jesus and being present with Him. While Martha was running around, Mary was paying attention to Jesus. While Martha was doing good things, Mary was doing the best thing she could do—focusing on Jesus.

**What is the best thing you can do for your marriage?**

The answer is, the same thing Mary did: focus on Jesus.

Some marriages suffer from what we might call Martha Disorder. One of the symptoms is distraction. (See v. 40.)

**What are some common distractions that keep you and your spouse from focusing on Jesus?**

Another symptom of Martha Disorder is worry (see v. 41).

**If we trust that God is faithful and in control, then why do we worry?**

"Regardless of how convinced we are, God has not placed us in control of our environments nor are we responsible for how everyone is behaving or how things will turn out. He is still God and, yes, even over 'this,' whatever your 'this' may be."
**—BETH MOORE[2]**

One day, Shirley walked into the room when I was watching TV. She started talking to me about something, but I wasn't paying attention. She could tell I wasn't paying attention, quit talking, and left the room. I apologized and gave her my full attention.

Isn't that how we treat God sometimes? We are focused on something else, and God is desiring for our attention. That "something else" may not be a bad thing, but can cause us to ignore or neglect God. Our worries and priorities can take the place of God in our lives.

**What can you and your spouse do to make sure that your marriage relationship stays focused on Jesus?**

The solution to worry is daily surrender to Jesus.

● **READ** Luke 9:23:

> Then He said to them all, "If anyone wants to come with Me, he must deny himself, take up his cross daily, and follow Me."

**How do Jesus' words speak to you about your tendency to worry?**

**What differences would we see in our world if more spouses denied themselves, took up their crosses, and followed Jesus daily and passionately?**

## THIS WEEK'S INSIGHTS
• • •

- Too much busyness doing good things sometimes causes us to miss the best thing God has for us.
- Running on empty places stress on any marriage, while setting aside time together as a couple refreshes and restores.
- Spending time with Jesus every day helps couples refocus their priorities and make better use of their time.

We all have the same number of hours and days. Take some action to reduce stress at home.

Look with your spouse at calendars and eliminate at least one item from your schedule so the two of you can spend that time together. Be ready to share your experience with your group next week.

## WRAP UP
• • •

**THE PSALMS** are filled with prayers that direct God's people to focus on and praise Him in all circumstances. David's prayer in Psalm 86 is an excellent example. Read Psalm 86 and devote a few moments to praising God for His goodness, grace, and love.

Lord, You know how needy I am and how grateful
I am for Your graciousness, protection, and
faithfulness. You, Lord, are kind and ready to forgive,
rich in faithful love to all who call on You.
Lord, hear my prayer today. There is no other
like You and I praise You; thank You for wanting
a personal relationship with me. Teach me
Your ways and give me courage to obey.

● **READ AND COMPLETE** the following activities for this section before your next group time.

# MARITAL BONDING: AN EMOTIONAL COVENANT

Married partners often define romantic love in different ways. A woman is inclined to associate romance not just with the bedroom, but with the things a man does throughout the day and week to make her feel loved, protected, and respected. A man who shares in the duties of cooking, cleaning, and picking up the kids after basketball practice is much more likely to win the affection of his wife.

Men rely more on their senses. They appreciate a wife who makes herself as attractive as possible. A man also wants to be respected and admired by his wife. He likes to hear his wife express genuine interest in his opinions, hobbies, and work. He loves to "overhear" her bragging about him to her friends.

Song of Songs includes this eloquent description of the connection between two married lovers: "Love is as strong as death, its jealousy unyielding as the grave. It burns like blazing fire, like a mighty flame"(8:6). This fiery, romantic sexually intimate love is not achieved overnight. It develops between a man and a woman through a process called *marital bonding*. Such bonding refers to the emotional covenant that links a man and a woman together for life and makes them intensely valuable to one another. It is this specialness that sets those two lovers apart from every other couple on the face of the earth. It is God's gift of intimate companionship.

According to research of Dr. Desmond Morris, bonding is most likely to develop among those who have moved systematically and slowly through twelve steps during their courtship and early marriage. The following stages represent the progression of physical intimacy from which a permanent commitment often evolves: (1) Eye to body, (2) eye to eye, (3) voice to voice, (4) hand to hand, (5) hand to shoulder,

(6) hand to waist, (7) face to face, (8), Hand to head, (9) hand to body, (10) mouth to breast, (11) touching below the waist, and (12) intercourse.[3] The final four steps of physical contact should be reserved for the marital relationship since they are progressively sexual and intensely personal.

When two people love each other deeply and are committed for life, they have usually developed a great volume of understanding between them that would be considered insignificant to anyone else. They share countless private memories unknown to the rest of the world.

The critical factor is that they have taken these steps *in sequence*. When later stages are reached prematurely, such as when couples kiss passionately on the first date or have sexual intercourse before marriage, something precious is lost from the relationship.

This bonding concept does not apply only to courtship experiences. The most successful marriages are those in which husbands and wives regularly journey through the twelve steps to physical intimacy regularly. Touching and talking and holding hands and gazing into one another's eyes and building memories are as important to partners in their midlife years as to newlyweds in their twenties.

Indeed, the best way to invigorate a tired sex life is to walk through the twelve steps regularly and with gusto!

Read and talk about this article with your spouse. Which were new insights for you? For your spouse?

# A PRESCRIPTION FOR
# MARTHA DISORDER

Are you and your spouse going to suffer from the distraction and worry caused by Martha Disorder, or will you stay focused on Jesus?

**1. TRUST JESUS AS YOUR FAITHFUL SHEPHERD.** A shepherd's role is to protect, provide, and guide. Jesus is saying: "If you will trust Me as your shepherd, then I will take care of you. I will meet your needs. I will protect you from the enemy. And I will lead you faithfully through all circumstances." Are you and your spouse listening to His voice?

Set aside time this week to read John 10:11-18, in which Jesus talks about His role as shepherd.

> **Why is it important to understand that Jesus did not have to die, but that He voluntarily chose to lay down His life for you (see v. 18)?**

**2. LET PRAYER DRIVE EVERY AREA OF YOUR LIFE.** If you have children, you love to be connected to them. You love it when your children come to you, talk to you, and trust you. In the same way, God loves to hear from us, His children. He wants you and your spouse to trust Him and express that trust through prayer.

● **READ** Philippians 4:6-7.

> **Why should we pray about everything?**

> **What are the results of a prayer-driven life? How have you and your spouse seen God work in your marriage through prayer?**

# DEALING WITH FATIGUE
# AND TIME PRESSURE

Here are three ideas for respecting each other and guarding against the overcommitted life.

1. Most of us can tolerate stresses and pressure much more easily if at least one other person knows we are experiencing it. The frustrations of our responsibilities will be much more manageable if our spouses communicate that they understand and appreciate all we have done. Even if our husband or wife can do nothing to change the situation, simply their acknowledgment that we did an admirable job today will make it easier for us to repeat the assignment tomorrow.

   Everyone needs to know that they are respected for the way they handle responsibilities. Working spouses get this emotional nurture through job promotions, pay raises, annual evaluations, and incidental praise during the workday. Those at home get affirmation from their spouse. Fulfilled and energized spouses feel understood and cherished, even in the midst of fatigue and time pressure.

2. Most men and women agree that the daily tasks of running a household can be managed; it is the accumulating projects that seem to overwhelm. Periodically, someone has to clean the stove and refrigerator, and replace the shelf paper, clean the gutters, trim the hedges, and clean the windows. These kinds of responsibilities are cyclical and can prevent them from ever feeling caught up.

   Though it is rarely possible for a busy family, everyone needs to do things every now and then that may not seem important, but inspire hobbies, creativity, and passion for life. But the entire world seems to conspire against such reconstructive activities.

This list provides a simple prescription for a happier, healthier life, but it must be implemented by the individual family. You must resolve to confess your selfishness; slow your pace; learn to say no gracefully; resist temptation to chase after more commitments; and hold the line with the tenacity of a tackle for a professional football team, blocking out intruders and defending the home team.

> **What is one action you might take this week to "block our intruders" or "defend the home team"?**

## PERSONAL REFLECTION
• • •

Prayer is a way we stay surrendered to Jesus. When we don't pray, it's as if we are saying, "Jesus, we don't need you. We'll get back to you when we have a bigger problem."

> **Use this space to give priority as a couple to daily surrender to Him this week.**

1. American Psychological Association, *Stress in America: Our Health at Risk* [online], 11 January 2011 (cited 16 May 2014). Available from the Internet: *http://www.apa.org/news/press/releases/stress/2011/final-2011.pdf.*
2. Beth Moore, "Why Do You Worry?," *Living Proof Ministries Blog* [online] 1 June 2008 (cited 16 May 2014). Available from the Internet: *http://blog.lproof.org/2008/06/why-do-you-worry.html.*
3. Desmond Morris, *Intimate Behavior* (New York: Random House, 1971).

WEEK 3

# THE
# PRIORITY
· · · · · · · · · · · · · · · · · · · · · · · · · · ·
OF RELATIONSHIPS

● **START YOUR GROUP TIME** by discussing what participants discovered in their Reflect homework.

> How did you respond to the marital bonding principles in your home study this week?

> What did you delete from your schedule last week?

> What did you and your spouse do together instead?

> What difference did it make?

God put us on earth for relationships—with Him, with our spouse, our family and friends, and with other people.

> In the following quotation, which do you relate to most—the oil or the glue? Explain.

>> "Love is the glue that holds our marriages together and the oil that keeps us from rubbing each other the wrong way." (Patrick Morley, *Devotions for Couples*)[1]

Before you watch the video, pray together as a group. Thank God for what He is teaching you through this study.

● **WATCH CLIP 3** from the study DVD and answer the following questions. Watch for one action the Dobsons took to strengthen their marriage:

The day I described on video was the most meaningful day of my married life. It reinforced for me the need we all have for relationships, but most especially the one Shirley and I have.

> In the midst of all the demands on you, how do you make your relationship with your spouse a priority?

> Have the two of you had a getaway lately? How did your time together bring you closer?

> What did Shirley and I bring along on our day trip? What did we do to communicate with God?

Just as you pursue a healthy relationship with your spouse, so does your Heavenly Father pursue a healthy relationship with you. He wants to talk every day. He wants you to hear from His Word (the Bible) every day. He wants you to depend on Him for everything.

> Share some ways you are growing in your relationship with God.

> Why is it necessary to surround yourself with people who meet your need for authentic community and help you grow spiritually?

● **CONTINUE YOUR GROUP TIME** with this discussion guide.

Throughout Jesus' teaching ministry, He communicated the difference between having religion and having a relationship with God. A great example are His teachings in Matthew 22:36-40.

The religious leaders of his day established a religious system with more than 600 laws, and they devoted much of their time arguing over which commandments were more important.

One day, when Jesus was in their presence, the religious leaders huddled together and planned how they might humiliate Him in front of everybody. They chose the best and brightest from among them, a lawyer, and he asked Jesus a question, hoping that he might stump Him. Jesus was ready to respond.

## SIMPLY LOVE

● **READ** Matthew 22:36-40.

Jesus answered the lawyer's question with a command to love God.

> **What does Jesus mean when He commands us to love God with all our heart, soul, and mind?**

The second commandment also begins with love.

> **Who are your neighbors, and how do you love them like yourself? Specific to marriage, how do you love your spouse as you love yourself?**

**These commandments seem clear. Why do you think there are so many unhealthy relationships?**

Notice that Jesus put the two commandments together.

**Is it possible to separate loving God and loving other people? Why or why not?**

To love God with your heart, soul, and mind is to make Him the priority and treasure of your life. Loving God is where true life begins. Loving God means to know Him and to follow Him wholeheartedly. One way we show our love for God is by loving other people.

● **READ** Jesus' words in John 13:34-35.

**Recall some of the words and deeds of Jesus. How did He show His love for people?**

**Describe practical ways you can follow His example.**

We are to love one another just as Jesus has loved us. According to John 13:35, the people around us will know that we are Christ-followers if they see us loving one another.

Our friends are watching. Our coworkers are watching. Our children are watching. What if more churches were full of people who promoted love, unity, and grace? Can you only imagine the impact the church would have in our communities, nation, and world?

Your marriage should also be a visible picture of the love relationship between Christ and His church. (See Eph. 5:22-33.)

**What is it going to take for you and your spouse to display Christlike love to the world, starting at home?**

# MOTIVES MATTER

We can sing about God, serve in the church, help the poor, and go on a mission trip. But all of it needs to be done as an overflow of our love for Christ.

● **READ** 1 Corinthians 13:1-7.

**Based on these verses, what are the characteristics of love?**

**Why should love drive everything that we do?**

**Which characteristics do you see most reflected in your spouse? Which characteristics have room for improvement in your life?**

## THIS WEEK'S INSIGHTS

• • •

- Love is the foundation of all of our relationships.
- We cannot separate loving God from loving other people.
- Expressing our love for God and others should happen first and foremost in our marriage and home.
- The love Jesus described in Matthew 22 is a visible picture of the love relationship between Christ and His church.

What wisdom are you gaining from this study? Share what you are learning with another husband or wife not participating in the Bible study. If that person is not yet a Christian, ask God to open a door for you to tell them about your love for Christ.

## WRAP UP

• • •

**PRAY TOGETHER** by thanking God for His amazing love for you. Ask God to forgive you if you have not loved Him and others as you should. Ask for strength to be a person who loves like Jesus. Pray that God would give our group supernatural love for each other.

Dear God, May people know me by my love for
You and for them, and may this start first in my
home. Give me Your heart for loving people I
might not be able to love on my own. Help me to
be a loving neighbor in Jesus' name, Amen.

● **READ AND COMPLETE** the activities for this section before your next group time.

## CULTIVATING FOUR RELATIONSHIPS

According to Jesus, loving God and loving others go together. A couple who wants to obey these commandments and live the life God intended needs to cultivate four relationships.

**1. RELATIONSHIP WITH JESUS CHRIST.** No other relationship is more important than your relationship with Jesus Christ. God created us to know Him and follow Him. Jesus wants you to follow Him every day and in every area of life.

● **READ** Matthew 4:18-22.

What did Jesus invite these men to do? How did they respond?

These disciples began a relationship with Jesus that would allow them to talk with Jesus and learn from Him every day.

What are you doing to talk with Jesus and learn from Him every day?

**2. RELATIONSHIP WITH YOUR SPOUSE.** Your relationship with your spouse is your second most important relationship. When I travel, as I often do, I don't walk out of the house saying, "I'll talk to you when I get back!" No, Shirley and I talk on the phone every day that I'm away from home. Our relationship is a priority so it would be strange to even go one day without talking with her.

● **REVIEW** Ephesians 5:22-33. Also read 1 Peter 3:1-7.

What do these passages say about the role of the husband? The role of the wife? (You may want to look back at your responses in Week 1.) When husbands and wives fulfill their God-given roles, their relationship will grow stronger.

> **What are you doing to fulfill your role in order to develop your relationship with your spouse?**

**3. RELATIONSHIPS WITH OTHER CHRISTIANS.** Experiencing authentic community with other believers is crucial for your spiritual growth. Take the time to connect with a small group of Christ followers who will encourage you and challenge you to grow in your faith. The early Christians in the Book of Acts understood their need for community.

● **READ** Acts 2:42-47.

> **What do you notice about the commitment of these believers to each other?**

> **What are you doing to develop relationships with other Christians?**

**4. RELATIONSHIPS WITH PEOPLE WHO DO NOT FOLLOW CHRIST.** God created you for a mission. (See Matt. 28:18-20.) If you just focus on developing the other three relationships, you will miss out on that exciting mission.

Rick Warren offers couples the encouragement to care about people who do not know God yet: "The fact is, if you want God's blessing on your marriage, then you must care about what God cares about most. What is that? He wants his lost children found! He wants everyone to know Him and His purposes for their lives."[2]

**What are you doing to develop relationships with people who do not follow Christ?**

## GUARD AGAINST MARRIAGE KILLERS

Wise couples will always be on guard against marriage killers.

*Overcommitment and physical exhaustion*—It is especially dangerous for newly married. Do not try to go to college, work full-time, have a baby, manage a toddler, fix up a house, and start a business all at once. Spouses must reserve time for one another if they want to keep their love alive. (See Rom. 12:1-2; Ex. 20:8-10.)

*Excessive debt and conflict over how money is spent*—Allocate your resources with the wisdom of Solomon. Do not overcommit. (See Ps. 119:36; Prov. 21:5.)

*Selfishness*—You are selfish. It's a fact. Because of this, friction is too often the order of the day. Selfishness will devastate a marriage over time. (See Phil. 2:3.)

*Interference from in-laws*—If husbands or wives have not been fully emancipated from their parents, it is best not to live near them. (See Matt. 19:4-6.)

*Unrealistic expectations*—Some couples enter marriage anticipating rose-colored cottages, walks down primrose lanes, and uninterrupted joy. This illusion is true for both brides and grooms who expect more from their mates than they are capable of delivering. (See Phil. 4:8.)

*Space invaders*—My concern is for those who violate the breathing room needed by their partners, quickly suffocating them and destroying the attraction between them. Jealousy is one way this phenomenon expresses itself. (See Prov. 14:30.)

*Alcohol or drug abuse and other addictions*—Both alcohol and substance abuse are killers of people and marriages. It is impossible to play with these or other enticements like pornography and not get hurt. Few walk away unaffected. For some, there is a vulnerability that is not recognized until it is too late. (See 1 Pet. 2:11; 1 Cor. 6:12.)

*Sexual frustration, loneliness, low self-esteem, and the seemingly greener grass of infidelity*—A deadly combination! (See 1 Cor. 10:13.)

*Business success and business failure*—It is almost as risky to succeed wildly in business as it is to fail miserably. Failure does bad things, to men especially. Those who profit handsomely sometimes become drunk with power—and the lust for more. (See Jas. 3:13-17; Phil. 4:12-13.)

*Getting married too young*—Those who marry at eighteen or nineteen are one and a half times as likely to divorce as those who marry in their twenties. The pressures of adolescence and the stress of early married life do not mix well. (See Prov. 4:4-9.)

## DOING LIFE HAND IN HAND

We human beings can survive the most difficult of circumstances if we are not forced to stand alone. Women need men, and men need women, and that's the way God created us. He said it is "not good for the man to be alone" (Gen. 2:18).

When the family conforms to God's design, each member knows of his or her value because he or she is created in the image of God. This brings true contentment and worth—which satisfies romantic aspirations— which abolishes loneliness, isolation, and boredom— which contributes to sexual fulfillment—which binds the marriage together in fidelity—which provides security for children—which gives parents a sense of purpose—which contributes to self-esteem once more. The chain has no weak links.

What do women most want from their husbands, and what do men most want from their wives? Not a bigger home or better vacations, or a newer automobile. We all want the assurance that hand in hand we'll face the best and worst that life has to offer—together.

## PERSONAL REFLECTION
• • •

Love covers it all, doesn't it? The daily stresses on marriage, the most difficult situations—Christlike love is the answer. You, Lord, are the source of love.

**Pray that He will help us guard against marriage killers as a couple.**

1. Patrick Morley, *Devotions for Couples—Man in the Mirror Edition: For Busy Couples Who Want More Intimacy in Their Relationships* (Grand Rapids: Zondervan, 1998), 151.
2. Rick Warren, "The Purpose-Driven Marriage," *Today's Christian Woman* [online], September 2008 (cited 16 May 2014). Available from the Internet: *http://www.todayschristianwoman.com/articles/2008/september/purpose-driven-marriage.html*.

# FINANCIAL
# **FIDELITY**

● **START YOUR GROUP TIME** by discussing what participants discovered in their Reflect homework.

Last week you were asked to consider some potential marriage killers, as well as four vital relationships.

> How would strengthening these relationships offer some protection against marriage killers? Did you identify one relationship as needing attention?

> Did any of the marriage killers surprise you? Would you add anything else to the list?

> Many marriages face problems because of money issues. Why do you think this is the case?

An unfortunate reality for many couples is either the failure to communicate about finances or dysfunctional communication, such as one spouse lying to the other about spending habits.

Gail Saltz, a relationship expert and NBC News contributor, explains: "Lying to your partner about (money) is basically a kind of betrayal (and) diminishes the trust between you. Loss of trust usually ends a marriage. Financial infidelity can be as bad as sexual infidelity in terms of the hurt and destruction it causes."[1]

● **WATCH CLIP 4** from the study DVD and answer the following questions:

> What are some ways we spend money, time, and energy in the hope of being satisfied?

> In your opinion, how do financial difficulties affect other areas of a marriage?

> What do you understand this statement to mean: "I have learned that everything that I own very quickly owns me"?

After more than fifty years of marriage, Shirley and I are still working together to make our lives less complicated. Would you consider making the same commitment for your family?

> In what ways might your family simplify life?

> We all know that money cannot buy happiness. Yet, how and why do so many people still seem to buy into the lie?

⬤ **CONTINUE YOUR GROUP TIME** with this discussion guide.

Several years ago a *U.S. News and World Report* article addressed the tendency to make bad choices even when we know better: "Part of it is that we are wired to care more about immediate, tangible consequences than about delayed and intangible consequences. ... If we buy a $5 latte now, we get immediate pleasure, but the long-term impact on our goal to have half a million dollars when we retire is minute."[2]

Money problems and poor financial decisions can occur when a husband and wife are only thinking short term.

⬤ **READ** Isaiah 55:2-3.

The people Isaiah described were spending their money and energy on things that did not matter. As these verses clearly state, we need to "come" to God, listen, and accept His gracious invitation and free gift.

> **When we come to Him, what does He promise? (See v. 3.) Why should that promise be enough to satisfy?**

It is extremely important for husbands and wives to develop a biblical understanding of money in order to fulfill God's purposes with the money He has "loaned" them.

At least four truths comprise such a biblical perspective. For each one, rate yourself 1-10 for the extent to which you and your spouse live by this truth (*1 Never think about it* to *10 Evaluate all financial decisions by this truth*).

**1. TRUTH: GOD IS THE OWNER OF ALL OF YOUR MONEY. _____**
In 1 Chronicles 29, King David encouraged the people to support the building of the temple. The people accepted his challenge, and David responded with a prayer of praise.

● **READ** a portion of David's prayer in 1 Chronicles 29:11-16.

> What do these verses say about the nature and character of God? About the people of God?

What we believe about the nature and character of God is foundational for what we do with the money He has so graciously loaned us.

● **READ** 1 Corinthians 6:19-20.

While Paul was addressing the Corinthians about sexual immorality, his words apply to all areas of life, including financial stewardship. We do not belong to ourselves, but have been "bought at a price" (v. 20).

> If we lived as though we belonged to God, glorifying God in our spending, how would we use the money He has loaned us?

**2. TRUTH: GOD WANTS YOUR HEART. _____**
God doesn't need our money; He is the owner of it all. God wants us to have freedom *from* the love of money (see Heb. 13:5) and freedom *to* serve Him exclusively. (See Matt. 4:8-10.)

● **READ** Matthew 6:24.

> Why is it impossible to serve God and money?

Many people are driven by their finances, thinking that more money will bring them security. However, money and possessions are temporary, often disappearing quickly. Lasting security can only be found in a relationship with God, who desires our devotion.

**3. TRUTH: GENEROUS GIVING IS A SPIRITUAL DISCIPLINE THAT GROWS YOUR FAITH AND DIRECTS YOUR HEART. _____**

● **READ** 1 Timothy 4:7-8.

> How much attention should we give to spiritual training?

If you have trained for a marathon, you know the discipline required. These verses instruct to "train yourself in godliness." Giving is a spiritual discipline that helps make you more like Christ.

> What are some benefits of making the discipline of giving a priority in your marriage?

● **READ** Jesus' words in Matthew 6:19-21.

How you and your spouse use money is not only a reflection of your heart, it also influences the direction of your heart.

> How can husbands and wives put this principle into practice so their hearts are where God desires?

**4. TRUTH: GOD IS FAITHFUL TO MEET ALL YOUR NEEDS. _____**
The apostle Paul told the Christians at Philippi that God was pleased with their financial support of him and his work. He then reminded them of God's faithful provision in their lives. (See Phil. 4.)

● **READ** Philippians 4:19.

> What would marriages look like if couples really believed that God would supply all their needs?

## THIS WEEK'S INSIGHTS

• • •

- God is the owner of our money, and He is faithful to meet all of our needs.
- Our giving reflects the attitude and actions of our heart.
- Lasting security can only be found in a relationship with God.
- Generous giving can be developed as a spiritual discipline.

In healthy marriages, couples look for ways to grow and mature in their faith. Excellent Bible studies, including others in the *Dobson Building a Family Legacy* series, are available for another small-group Bible study. Visit *www.lifeway.com* and search "Bible study" or "small groups" or "Dobson" for studies of interest. Pray about what is next for you, and then commit to do it.

**How will we continue to grow as a couple and strengthen our marriage?**

## WRAP UP

• • •

**PRAY TOGETHER** around the four giving truths and other insights from this study. Acknowledge God as the owner of everything. Surrender your heart to Him and His purposes. Ask God to help you develop the discipline of giving in your marriage.

Loving God, we trust You to meet all of our needs.
Thank You for Your gracious provision, and help
our family be people of generosity and grace.

● **READ AND COMPLETE** the activities for this section before your next group time.

## EMPTY CASTLES

Once, during a trip to England, I was dramatically reminded of the folly of materialism. As I toured beautiful museums and historical buildings, I was struck by what I called "empty castles." Standing there in the lonely fog were the edifices constructed by proud men who thought they owned them. But where are those men today?

Time is like a well-greased string that slides through our fingers. So there is no better time than now for you and me to assess the values that are worthy of our time and effort.

When I reach the end of my days, a moment or two from now, I must look back on something more meaningful than the pursuit of homes and land and stocks and bonds and fame. I will consider my earthly existence to have significance only if I can recall a loving family, a consistent investment in the lives of people, and an earnest attempt to serve the God who made me.

## A TALE OF TWO MONEY MEN: A CLOSER LOOK AT GENEROSITY

Examine in the Bible two powerful stories about men with money—stories with completely different endings. One man walked away from Jesus while the other one began to follow Him. One remained selfish with his stuff while the other became a generous giver. Money ruled one man while Jesus ruled the other man.

**THE RICH YOUNG RULER—**This rich guy was not a follower of Jesus, but he knew about Jesus and set out to ask Him a very important question—a question people today still ask in various ways.

● **READ** Mark 10:17-22.

What did this man ask? How would you answer?

Why do you think Jesus rebuked the young man for calling Him "good" (v. 18)?

What does this story tell you about the heart of Jesus? Of the rich young ruler? What is a key lesson you learn from this story?

Sadly, this young man missed out on the opportunity of a lifetime because he allowed his money to master him.

**ZACCHAEUS**—Day-by-day this rich tax collector was busy doing his job and building his bank account. But one day, Zacchaeus heard that someone named Jesus was coming to town. He would never be the same.

● **READ** Luke 19:1-10.

Why do you think Jesus said He "must stay" with Zacchaeus (v. 5)? How did Zacchaeus respond?

According to verse 8, what did Zacchaeus decide to do with his money? What do you learn from him?

Clearly Jesus had a divine plan for Zacchaeus.

> **How do you respond when you reflect on the fact that Jesus has a divine plan for you?**

Zacchaeus went from being a cheating tax collector to a generous giver, from self-righteousness to servanthood. And it all started with this defining moment when Jesus captured his heart and changed his life.

Perhaps, in recent weeks, God has used people and circumstances to capture your heart and challenge you to surrender to Him. Defining moments demand a decision. Today may be when you surrender every area of your life to Christ, including finances.

Maybe you've been a Christian for years, but your faith has been on cruise control. You're a comfortable Christian, but you're not really living the life of faith God desires. Maybe God is using this study to capture your heart and challenge you to surrender to Him.

The Bible says that Christ "died for all so that those who live should no longer live for themselves, but for the One who died for them and was raised" (2 Cor. 5:15). Jesus died for us so that we could live for Him in every way. If we surrender to Him every day, we will be the most generous people on earth.

## KNOW WHERE YOUR MONEY GOES

A consistent look at where your money goes will reveal family financial habits and areas in which you need to be more purposeful. This week set aside time as a couple to track monthly spending. Look closely at where your money is going. In the space provided or on extra pages, record the amount of money you spend every month. Add other categories as needed.

# MONTHLY SPENDING

| | |
|---|---|
| TOTAL INCOME | $_____ |

| | |
|---|---|
| GIVING TO CHURCH | _____% income |
| GIVING TO OTHER CHARITIES | _____% income |
| SAVINGS | _____% income |
| DEBT | _____% income |
| PERSONAL | |
| (food, housing, utilities, entertainment, etc.) | _____% income |
| DISCRETIONARY | _____% income |

**What do these percentages say about your priorities? What adjustments do you need to make in spending?**

# YOU CANNOT OUTGIVE GOD

I remember the day as though it were yesterday. The Dobsons had run out of money. There was no reserve to tide us over. My father gathered my mother and me in the bedroom for a time of prayer. He prayed first: "Oh, Lord, You promised that if we would be faithful to You and Your people in our good times, then You would not forget us in our time of need. We have tried to be generous with what You have given us, and now we are calling on You for help."

An impressionable ten-year-old boy named Jimmy was watching and listening. *What will happen?* he wondered. *Did God hear Dad's prayer?*

The next day an unexpected check for $1,200 came for us in the mail. Honestly! That's the way it happened, not just once but many times. God never made us wealthy, but my young faith grew by leaps and bounds. I learned that you cannot outgive God!

Because of its significance in God's kingdom (see Heb. 10:24-25; Eph. 3:10), your local church should be at the top of your giving. But may I also urge you to give generously to the needy people God puts in your path? You can hardly remain selfish or greedy when you are busy sharing what you have with others.

## FUTURE GIVING

| ORGANIZATION/CHARITY | WHY I GIVE | AMOUNT | % INCOME |
| --- | --- | --- | --- |
| *Now* | | | |
| *Future* | | | |

## PERSONAL REFLECTION

• • •

**Prayerfully consider your response to this quote as a couple:**

"We cannot follow two things. If Christ is one
of them, we cannot follow another. ...
Not only would it be very weakening to you to
attempt to serve both, but it is absolutely impossible
that you should do so. ... Christ must be everything
or He will be nothing." —Charles Spurgeon[3]

1.  "American Couples Have a Dirty Little Secret," *Today* [online], 27 December 2010 (cited 16 May 2014). Available from the Internet: *http://www.today.com/id/40794684/site/todayshow/ns/today-money/t/american-couples-have-dirty-little-secret/*.
2.  Adam Voiland, "Want to Break a Bad Habit? Try This," *Health* [online], 7 December 2007 (cited 16 May 2014). Available from the Internet: *http://health.usnews.com/health-news/articles/2007/12/07/want-to-break-a-bad-habit-try-this*.
3.  Charles Spurgeon, "The One Thing Necessary" [online] (cited 16 May 2014). Available from the Internet: *http://www.spurgeongems.org/vols16-18/chs1015.pdf*.

# Key Insights

## WEEK 1
- Husbands and wives have distinctive God-ordained roles and responsibilities in marriage.
- Submission means yielding one's rights for another person.
- Husbands are to love sacrificially and lead spiritually, following Christ's example as head of the church.
- Wives are to give themselves to their husbands, respecting and meeting their needs, just as the church submits to Christ. They find encouragement in their husband's affirmation and support.

## WEEK 2
- Too much busyness doing good things sometimes causes us to miss the best thing God has for us.
- Running on empty places stress on any marriage, while setting aside time together as a couple refreshes and restores.
- Spending time with Jesus every day helps couples refocus their priorities and make better use of their time.

## WEEK 3
- Love is the foundation of all of our relationships.
- We cannot separate loving God from loving other people.
- Expressing our love for God and others should happen first and foremost in our marriage and home.
- The love Jesus described in Matthew 22 is a visible picture of the love relationship between Christ and His church.

## WEEK 4
- God is the owner of our money, and He is faithful to meet all of our needs.
- Our giving reflects the attitude and actions of our heart.
- Lasting security can only be found in a relationship with God.
- Generous giving can be developed as a spiritual discipline.

# Leader Notes

It's time for a leadership adventure. Don't worry: you don't have to have all the answers. You're just here to facilitate the group discussion, getting participants back on topic when they stray, encouraging all members to share honestly and authentically, and also guiding those who might dominate the conversation to make sure others are getting some time to share.

As facilitator, take time to look over the entire study guide, noting the order and requirements of each session. Watch all the videos as well. Take time to read the suggested chapters (noted in the beginning of each Reflect section) from the book *Love for a Lifetime* (ISBN 978-1-4964-0328-5). And pray over the material, the participants, and your time together.

You have the option of extending your group's study by showing the films *Love for a Lifetime* and *Your Legacy*. You can also keep it to four weeks by using just this study guide and DVD. The study is easy to customize for your group's needs.

Go over the How to Use This Study and the Guidelines for Groups sections with your group, making members aware of best practices and the steps of each session. Then dive into Week 1.

In establishing a schedule for each group meeting, consider ordering the following elements as such for the hour of time together:

1. Connect—10 minutes
2. Watch—15 minutes
3. Engage—35 minutes

Be sure to allow time during each session to show the video clip. All four clips are approximately eight minutes or less in length. Reflect refers to the home study or activities done between group sessions.

Beginning with session 2, encourage some sharing regarding the previous week's Reflect home study. Usually at least one Connect question allows for this interaction. Sharing about the previous week's activities encourages participants to study on their own and be ready to share with their group during the next session.

As the study comes to a close, consider some ways to keep in touch. There may be some additional studies for which group members would like information. Some may be interested in knowing more about your church.

Occasionally, a group member may have needs that fall outside the realm of a supportive small group. If someone would be better served by the pastoral staff at your church or a professional counselor, please gather a list of professionals to privately offer to that person, placing his/her road to recovery in the hands of a qualified pastor or counselor.

Use the space below to make notes or to identify specific page numbers and questions you would like to discuss with your small group each week based on their needs and season of life.

# Further Resources

Need more guidance? Check out the following for help.

**MARRIAGE**

*HomeLife* magazine

*ParentLife* magazine

*The Five Love Languages: How to Express Heartfelt Commitment to Your Mate* by Dr. Gary Chapman

*Love and Respect: The Love She Most Desires, the Respect He Desperately Needs* by Emerson Eggerichs

*What the Bible Says About Love, Marriage, and Sex* by David Jeremiah

*Experiencing God at Home* by Richard Blackaby and Tom Blackaby

*The Love Dare* journal and *The Love Dare Bible Study* by Michael Catt, Stephen Kendrick, and Alex Kendrick

*The Love Dare for Parents Bible Study* by Stephen Kendrick and Alex Kendrick

*The Resolution for Men* by Randy Alcorn, Stephen Kendrick, and Alex Kendrick

*The Resolution for Women* by Priscilla Shirer

*Intimacy: Understanding a Woman's Heart* by Kenny Luck

*For Married Women Only: Three Principles for Honoring Your Husband* by Tony Evans

*Men Are Like Waffles, Women Are Like Spaghetti: Understanding and Delighting in Your Differences* by Bill and Pam Farrel

*The Secret to the Marriage You Want: The Trading Places Small Group Experience* by Les and Leslie Parrott

*Extraordinary Marriage: God's Plan for Your Journey* by Rodney and Selma Wilson

*For Women Only: The Bible Study: What You Need to Know About the Inner Lives of Men* by Shaunti Feldhahn

*For Young Women Only* by Shaunti Feldhahn and Lisa A. Rice

*For Men Only Discussion Guide: A Companion to the Bestseller About the Inner Lives of Women* by Jeff Feldhahn, Shaunti Feldhahn, and Brian Smith

# Introducing Your Child to Christ

Your most significant calling and privilege as a parent is to introduce your children to Jesus Christ. A good way to begin this conversation is to tell them about your own faith journey.

Outlined below is a simple gospel presentation you can share with your child. Define any terms they don't understand and make it more conversational, letting the Spirit guide your words and allowing your child to ask questions and contribute along the way.

**GOD RULES.** The Bible tells us God created everything, and He's in charge of everything. (See Gen. 1:1; Col. 1:16-17; Rev. 4:11.)

**WE SINNED.** We all choose to disobey God. The Bible calls this sin. Sin separates us from God and deserves God's punishment of death. (See Rom. 3:23; 6:23.)

**GOD PROVIDED.** God sent Jesus, the perfect solution to our sin problem, to rescue us from the punishment we deserve. It's something we, as sinners, could never earn on our own. Jesus alone saves us. (See John 3:16; Eph. 2:8-9.)

**JESUS GIVES.** He lived a perfect life, died on the cross for our sins, and rose again. Because Jesus gave up His life for us, we can be welcomed into God's family for eternity. This is the best gift ever! (See Rom. 5:8; 2 Cor. 5:21; Eph. 2:8-9; 1 Pet. 3:18.)

**WE RESPOND.** Believe in your heart that Jesus alone saves you through what He's already done on the cross. Repent, by turning away from your sin. Tell God and others that your faith is in Jesus. (See John 14:6; Rom. 10:9-10,13.)

If your child is ready to respond, explain what it means for Jesus to be Lord of his or her life. Guide your child to a time in prayer to repent and express his or her belief in Jesus. If your child responds in faith, celebrate! You now have the opportunity to disciple your child to be more like Christ.

**YOUR LEGACY**
BIBLE STUDY
THE GREATEST GIFT
DR. JAMES DOBSON

**BRINGING UP BOYS**
BIBLE STUDY
SHAPING THE NEXT GENERATION OF MEN
DR. JAMES DOBSON

**BRINGING UP GIRLS**
BIBLE STUDY
SHAPING THE NEXT GENERATION OF WOMEN
DR. JAMES DOBSON

THE
**STRONG-WILLED CHILD**
BIBLE STUDY
SURVIVING BIRTH THROUGH ADOLESCENCE
DR. JAMES DOBSON

# BUILD YOUR FAMILY LEGACY.

**DARE TO DISCIPLINE**
BIBLE STUDY
ANSWERS TO YOUR TOUGHEST PARENTING QUESTIONS
DR. JAMES DOBSON

**LOVE FOR A LIFETIME**
BIBLE STUDY
BUILDING A MARRIAGE THAT WILL GO THE DISTANCE
DR. JAMES DOBSON

**STRAIGHT TALK TO MEN**
BIBLE STUDY
TIMELESS PRINCIPLES FOR LEADING YOUR FAMILY
DR. JAMES DOBSON

**WANTING TO BELIEVE**
BIBLE STUDY
FAITH, FAMILY, AND FINDING AN EXCEPTIONAL LIFE
RYAN DOBSON

Dr. James Dobson leads you through his classic messages and new insights for today's families in these eight DVD-based Bible studies. Each Building a Family Legacy Bible study includes four-sessions with personal reflection and discussion guides along with a DVD of Dr. Dobson's teachings, introduced by his son, Ryan. Studies include:

Your Legacy Bible Study
Bringing Up Boys Bible Study
Bringing Up Girls Bible Study
Dare to Discipline Bible Study
The Strong-Willed Child Bible Study
Straight Talk to Men Bible Study
Love for a Lifetime Bible Study
Wanting to Believe Bible Study

*Learn more at LifeWay.com/Legacy*

Dr. James Dobson's **BUILDING A FAMILY LEGACY** campaign includes films, Bible studies, and books designed to help families of all ages and stages. Dr. Dobson's wisdom, insight, and humor promise to strengthen marriages and help parents meet the remarkable challenges of raising children. Most importantly, **BUILDING A FAMILY LEGACY** will inspire parents to lead their children to personal faith in Jesus Christ.

*Learn more at*

BUILDINGAFAMILYLEGACY.COM

# BUILDING A FAMILY LEGACY BOOKS

## From Dr. James Dobson and Tyndale Momentum

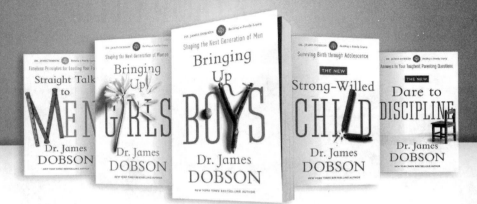

**BRINGING UP BOYS** • 978-1-4143-9133-5
Also available in hardcover (978-0-8423-5266-6) and audio CDs
(978-0-8423-2297-3)

**BRINGING UP GIRLS** • 978-1-4143-9132-8
Also available in hardcover (978-1-4143-0127-3) and audio CDs
read by Dr. James Dobson (978-1-4143-3650-3)

**THE NEW STRONG-WILLED CHILD** • 978-1-4143-9134-2
Also available in hardcover (978-0-8423-3622-2) and audio
CDs (978-0-8423-8799-6), as well as *The New Strong-Willed
Child Workbook* (978-1-4143-0382-6)

**THE NEW DARE TO DISCIPLINE** • 978-1-4143-9135-9

**STRAIGHT TALK TO MEN** • 978-1-4143-9131-1

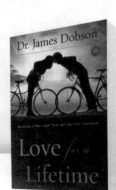

## AVAILABLE IN 2015

**LOVE FOR A LIFETIME**
Revised and expanded edition
978-1-4964-0328-5